Cambridge **Discovery Education**™
▶ **INTERACTIVE READERS**

Series editor: Bob Hastings

EMPIRE
RISE AND FALL

A2

Nic Harris

CAMBRIDGE
UNIVERSITY PRESS

Discovery
EDUCATION™

CAMBRIDGE
UNIVERSITY PRESS

University Printing House, Cambridge CB2 8BS, United Kingdom

One Liberty Plaza, 20th Floor, New York, NY 10006, USA

477 Williamstown Road, Port Melbourne, VIC 3207, Australia

4843/24, 2nd Floor, Ansari Road, Daryaganj, Delhi – 110002, India

79 Anson Road, #06–04/06, Singapore 079906

Cambridge University Press is part of the University of Cambridge.

It furthers the University's mission by disseminating knowledge in the pursuit of education, learning and research at the highest international levels of excellence.

www.cambridge.org
Information on this title: www.cambridge.org/9781107628441

First published 2014
20 19 18 17 16 15 14 13 12 11 10 9 8 7 6 5

Printed in Dubai by Oriental Press

A catalogue record for this publication is available from the British Library

Library of Congress Cataloging in Publication Data

Harris, Nicholas.
  Empire: rise and fall / Nic Harris.
    pages cm. — (Cambridge discovery interactive readers)
  ISBN 978-1-107-62844-1 (pbk. : alk. paper)
1. Civilization, Ancient—Juvenile literature. 2. English language—Textbooks for foreign speakers.
3. Readers (Elementary) I. Title.

CB311.H328 2014
930—dc23

                           2013014260

ISBN 978-1-107-62844-1

Additional resources for this publication at www.cambridge.org

Cambridge University Press has no responsibility for the persistence or accuracy of URLs for external or third-party internet websites referred to in this publication, and does not guarantee that any content on such websites is, or will remain, accurate or appropriate.

Layout services, art direction, book design, and photo research: Q2ABillSMITH GROUP
Editorial services: Hyphen S.A.
Audio production: CityVox, New York
Video production: Q2ABillSMITH GROUP

Contents

Before You Read:
Get Ready!

Complete the sentences with the correct words.

soldier   calendar   monument   tomb   government

1 People visit and take photos of this beautiful _____.

2 A _____ sometimes has to kill other people for his or her country.

3 A _____ is a group of very important people. Most countries have one.

4 A _____ shows us dates and months.

5 People put dead bodies in a _____.

Words to Know

Read the paragraph. Then complete the sentences with the correct highlighted words.

A lot of soldiers together are called an army. Almost every country in the world has an army. Sometimes, the soldiers attack and kill the soldiers of another country. When this happens, the two countries have a war. The country that wins sometimes takes control of the country that loses. The winning country can then tell the other country what it can and can't do. In the past, the country that lost sometimes became part of the country that won. When this happened, it was called a colony. When a country had a lot of colonies, it had an empire.

1. Those dogs are very dangerous. They often _____ people.

2. For many years, India didn't have its own government. It was a _____ of Britain.

3. There was a big _____ between 1939 and 1945. Many people died.

4. In the year 117, the Roman _____ included places from modern-day England to Egypt.

5. There are about 200,000 soldiers in the British _____.

6. A good teacher _____ of her class as soon as she arrives.

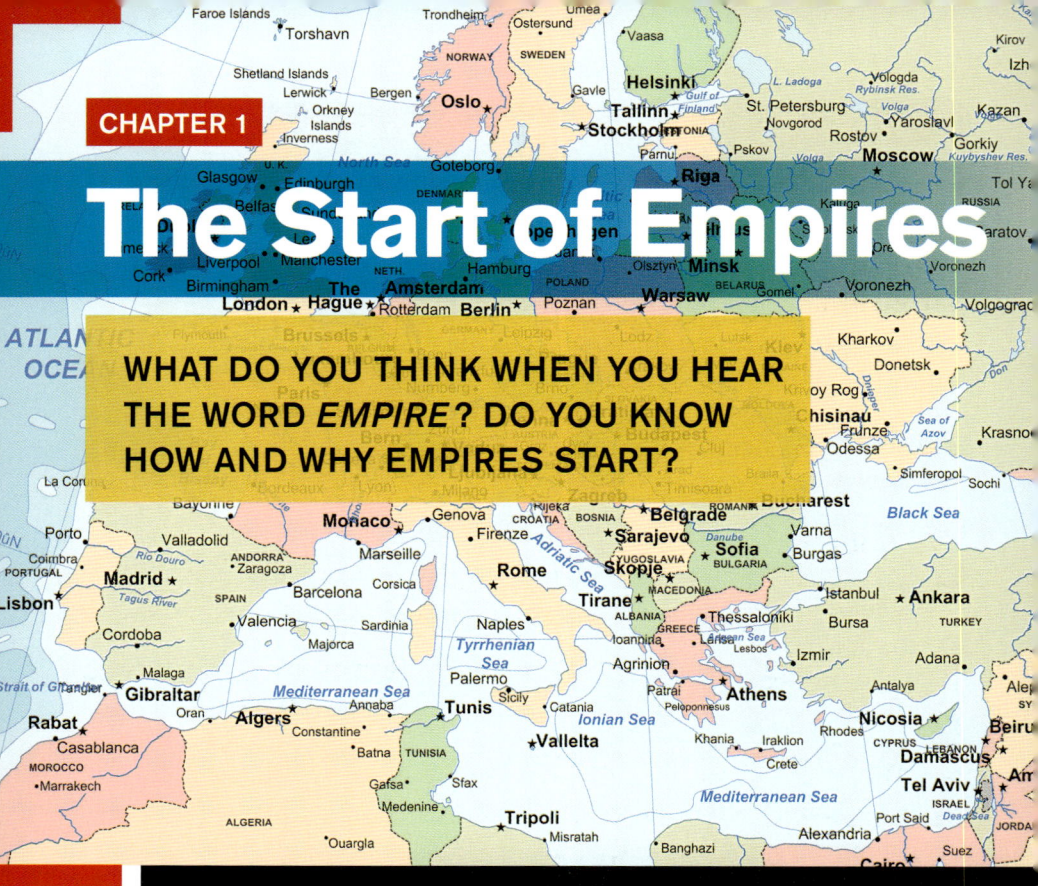

CHAPTER 1

The Start of Empires

WHAT DO YOU THINK WHEN YOU HEAR THE WORD *EMPIRE*? DO YOU KNOW HOW AND WHY EMPIRES START?

If you look at a map of the world today, you will see there are hundreds of countries. Each country has its own way of life, and many have their own languages.

Many thousands of years ago, the world was a very different place. In the beginning, there were no countries. People lived together in small groups. These groups were called tribes, and they were always moving around looking for food.

Then, about 12,000 years ago, people began to grow their own food and build houses. They began to use money. The strongest people usually became the **leaders** – the kings and queens.

The areas where they lived were their kingdoms. Over time, there were many kingdoms. Often, they joined together, and the kingdoms became very big.

The kingdoms did not always join together in a friendly way. Sometimes, a kingdom needed more food for its people. Or

Sometimes kingdoms attack others.

a king wanted more money. When this happened, a strong kingdom attacked others and took control of them. That was how empires started. An empire was a group of many kingdoms with one leader. The leader was called an emperor or an empress. He or she was the leader of millions of people.

There were many empires in different parts of the world at different times in the past. In this book, we are going to look at five of the most famous ones.

? PREDICT

Think about the Roman, British, Mayan, Egyptian, and Chinese empires. Which was the biggest? Which was the oldest? What are they famous for?

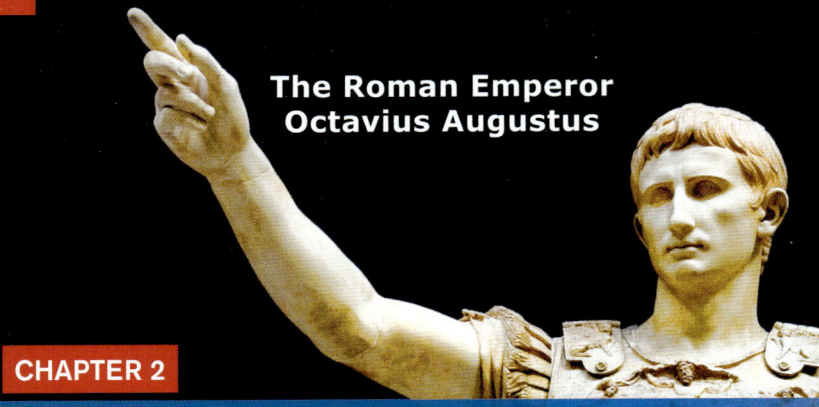

The Roman Emperor
Octavius Augustus

CHAPTER 2

The Roman Empire

EVERYBODY KNOWS THE NAME OF THE ROMANS. BUT DO YOU KNOW WHAT THEY GAVE TO THE WORLD?

The **ancient** Romans lived in modern-day Italy. They were very smart people and made one of the biggest, most important empires in the history of the world. The center of their empire was the city of Rome. The leaders of Rome took control of place after place until they had a very large empire. The first Roman emperor was a man called Octavius Augustus. He became emperor in 27 BCE.

At one time, 130 million people lived in the Roman Empire, and it was more than five million square kilometers in size.

There were about 130 emperors in the history of the empire. Many were good men. Augustus, for example, made sure there were very few wars, and he made the empire very rich. But other emperors were very bad, even crazy. It is difficult to be sure about things that happened so long ago, but there are many stories of crazy things that emperors did. People said that the Emperor Caligula wanted his horse to be in the government. They also said that Emperor Nero played a musical instrument while there was a big fire in Rome and people died.

People in every part of the Roman Empire knew what the emperor looked like. They saw his face all the time. The Romans put a picture of the emperor on their coins. This changed the way that people used money. People could buy things in any part of the empire with the same coins.

Roman coins

Life in the empire was good for the rich, important people, but it was terrible for regular people. In Rome there is a building called the Colosseum. It is like a stadium. Today, many people visit it and take pictures. But terrible things happened there. Thousands of people in ancient Rome came there to watch special sports. The sports were bloody and deadly. People had to **fight** and kill each other, or dangerous animals attacked and killed people. The Romans shouted happily as they watched.

The Colosseum in Rome

There were also many **slaves** in ancient Rome. A slave is someone who must work for a rich person, but doesn't get any money.

A lot of the things we use today came from the Romans. The Romans spoke Latin, and there are many Latin words in modern English and other European languages. They gave us the calendar we use today. They also built good roads. We can still see many Roman roads in Europe today!

So, what happened to the Romans? In the fifth century CE, the Roman Empire ended. There were many reasons for this:

- It was too big – it became more and more difficult for Rome to control it.

- The army was not as strong as before.

- The empire spent too much money, more than it had.

- It had **enemies**, most importantly, the Visigoths. This was a tribe from Germany. In 410 CE, the Visigoths attacked the city of Rome and brought the great Roman Empire to an end.

?

EVALUATE

Why do you think Romans liked to go to the Colosseum? Is there anything like this today?

Map of the world showing in red the extent of the British Empire in 1901

CHAPTER 3

The British Empire

WHEN IT WAS NIGHTTIME IN BRITAIN, IT WAS DAYTIME IN SOME PARTS OF THE BRITISH EMPIRE. THAT'S HOW BIG IT WAS!

The British Empire began in the early part of the 17th century. A small group of people traveled from England to live in what is now the USA. Later, a large part of North America and the Caribbean became part of the British Empire.

The British then looked toward[1] the East. In 1757, the British East India Company started to do business in India. In 1858, the British took control of India, and it became a colony. Many other countries like Canada, Hong Kong, Australia, and some countries in Africa also became colonies.

[1] **look toward:** be interested in

The British Empire was the biggest in the history of the world. In 1924, it was as big as Africa! And there were more than 450 million people living in it. That was almost a quarter of all the people living in the world at the time.

Like most empires, the British Empire did bad things and good things. It made money by selling African slaves in America. It killed **native** people in its colonies. It took natural resources[2] without paying for them. But it also built roads and railroads in the colonies that people still use today. And it brought the English language. Today, millions of people speak English as a first or a second language. It is now the international language of the world.

[2]**natural resource:** something from nature that people use, like wood, oil, or water

Wood

Water

Oil

? REMEMBER
Which parts of the world did the British take control of? Think about places where people speak English today.

CHAPTER 4

The Mayan Empire

THE MAYANS BUILT CITIES DEEP IN THE FORESTS OF CENTRAL AMERICA. THEN, SUDDENLY, THEY LEFT. NOBODY KNOWS WHY.

The Mayan people lived in the south of Mexico and parts of Central America. Their empire started about 2600 BCE and finished around 800 CE. It was about 250,000 square kilometers in size. That's not very big. In fact, it's about as big as Great Britain. They built many wonderful cities, and we can still see many of these today. The most famous is Chichén Itzá.

They bought and sold things with their neighbors. They were very good at this and made a lot of money. They were good doctors, too. Mayan doctors were called shamans, and they used plants to make medicines. There were even some Mayan dentists.

Chichén Itzá

The Mayans were very **religious** people. They believed in many gods, not just one. There were gods of the wind, of the rain, and of the sun. They even had a god of chocolate called *Ixcacao*. They built special buildings, temples, where they talked to their gods.

A Mayan temple

So what happened to the Mayans? Maybe they got sick and died. Maybe there was a terrible war. It is possible that they moved or died because they didn't have any food. Another answer could be the weather. Maybe it got too cold or too wet to live in their cities. But nobody knows for sure.

Video Quest

The Mayan Empire

Watch this video to learn about the Mayan city of Chichén Itzá. How many steps are there?

15

CHAPTER 5

The Egyptian Empire

THE PLACE THAT TIME DIDN'T FORGET. ITS WONDERFUL MONUMENTS ARE STILL HERE TODAY FOR EVERYBODY TO SEE.

The Egyptian Empire began around 3150 BCE and ended about 30 BCE, when the Roman Empire took control of it. At its strongest time, it included places from Syria to Sudan.

Kings and queens in ancient Egypt were called pharaohs. People believed the pharaohs were half human,[3] half god. When one of them died, they built a special **tomb** – a pyramid. They left money and food with the body so the pharaoh could use them in the next life.

[3] **human:** a person, not a thing, an animal, or a plant

They did another interesting thing with dead bodies – they made mummies! A mummy is a dead body with many pieces of cloth[4] around it. The cloth and special medicines preserved[5] the body.

Tutankhamen

In 1922, people found the body of an Egyptian pharaoh called Tutankhamen. He died when he was about 18, but his body is over 3,000 years old! You can still see the mummy in Tutankhamen's tomb today.

Ancient Egyptians were very good at math and science. They gave us many great things: a way to write language, a way to use numbers, paper, eye makeup, and even toothpaste to clean our teeth!

....

[4]**cloth:** what we use to make clothes, usually made from plants or animal hair

[5]**preserve:** keep something as it is naturally

Video Quest

The Egyptian Empire

Watch this video to learn about ancient Egyptian monuments. Why did they write on the walls?

CHAPTER 6

The Chinese Empire

QIN SHI HUANG MADE CHINA A COUNTRY, AN EMPIRE, AND AN INTERESTING PLACE TO VISIT, EVEN TODAY.

For many years, China was not one country. There were six kingdoms, and they were always having wars. Then in 221 BCE, a man called Qin Shi Huang took control and joined the kingdoms together. This was the beginning of the Chinese Empire.

Emperor Qin was worried about the kingdoms to the north of China, especially Mongolia. So, he started to build a very long wall between the two countries. The wall was 8,000 kilometers long at one time, and parts of it are still standing today.

Qin was also worried about the next life. He thought he might meet some bad people there. So, he made an army of more than 6,000 soldiers and put them in his tomb. But these were not real soldiers. They were made of terracotta, a kind of clay.

The terracotta army in Xi'an, China

The emperor wanted to live for many thousands of years. So, he told his doctors to make him a special drink. After drinking it, he died. Some say the doctors made a mistake, but some believe they wanted to kill the emperor.

Qin was emperor for only 12 years. However, he was an important man because he made China one empire. It stayed an empire for more than 2000 years. In 1922, the government changed and there were no more emperors. China is still a very strong country, but no longer an empire.

Video Quest

The Great Wall of China

Watch this video to learn about the Great Wall. When did they finish the wall?

CHAPTER 7

What Do You Think?

In this book you learned about ancient empires. But there are modern empires in the world today that did not come from kingdoms. Remember the two most important things about an empire: It has to be very big, and it has to have a leader that takes control of things.

This is a great idea. The food is very good and cheap, and the restaurants are very clean. Also, a lot of people will get jobs. And my community needs to be more international.

Think about the large businesses that are all over the world. They are also called empires – business empires. Do you think business empires are good or bad?

Let's look at one example.

Think about a small African town. There is a plan to open a fast-food restaurant there. Read what two people are saying about that plan. Which one do you agree with?

This is a terrible idea. Fast-food hamburgers can be very unhealthy. I don't want my children eating this food. They must eat African food. And the money we pay will go to the USA. Our money must stay in my community. My husband's restaurant will close because of this.

After You Read

Read the following sentences and choose Ⓐ, Ⓑ, or Ⓒ.

1 Slaves were people who worked _____.
- Ⓐ for fun
- Ⓑ but didn't get money
- Ⓒ for poor people

2 On each Roman coin, there was _____.
- Ⓐ a map of the empire
- Ⓑ a picture of an animal
- Ⓒ an emperor's face

3 The British Empire was the _____.
- Ⓐ largest in the world
- Ⓑ poorest in the world
- Ⓒ oldest in the world

4 The Mayans went to their temples and _____.
- Ⓐ played their favorite game
- Ⓑ talked to their gods
- Ⓒ bought and sold things

5 The pharaoh Tutankhamen died _____.
- Ⓐ when he was young
- Ⓑ in an accident
- Ⓒ during a war

6 The Egyptian Empire ended _____.
- Ⓐ when the last pharaoh died
- Ⓑ because the people didn't have enough food
- Ⓒ when the Romans took control of it

7 Qin was worried about his neighbors, so he _____.
- Ⓐ made an army out of terracotta
- Ⓑ drank bad medicine to kill himself
- Ⓒ built the Great Wall of China

Match the sentences with the correct empire (A–E). There are two sentences for each empire.

Ⓐ Roman   Ⓑ British   Ⓒ Mayan   Ⓓ Egyptian   Ⓔ Chinese

❶ Nobody knows why it ended.   _____

❷ India was part of it.   _____

❸ Six kingdoms joined together.   _____

❹ It lasted for more than 3000 years.   _____

❺ There were some very unusual emperors.   _____

❻ It had an army that didn't move.   _____

❼ It made money by selling African people as slaves. _____

❽ You can see the leader's dead body.   _____

❾ They had a god of something sweet.   _____

❿ There was a big fire in a city.   _____

? EVALUATE

Read the following sentences. Put a mark (✓) in the column to show whether you agree or disagree. Then give a reason.

	AGREE	DISAGREE	REASON
I would like my country to be part of an empire.			
There will be other famous empires in the future.			
I would like to have my own business empire.			

Answer Key

Words to Know, page 4

1 monument **2** soldier **3** government
4 calendar **5** tomb

Words to Know, page 5

1 attack **2** colony **3** war **4** Empire
5 Army **6** takes control

Predict, page 7

The biggest was the British Empire. The oldest was the
Egyptian Empire. They were all famous for many things.

Evaluate, page 11

Answers will vary.

Remember, page 13

It took control of the USA, a large part of North America,
the Caribbean, India, Canada, Hong Kong, Australia, and
some countries in Africa.

Video Quest, page 15

There are 365 steps to the top of the temple.

Video Quest, page 17

They wrote on the walls to give their pharaohs information
about the afterlife.

Video Quest, page 19

They finished the wall about 600 years ago.

Choose the Correct Answers, page 22

1 B **2** C **3** A **4** B **5** A **6** C **7** C

Match, page 23

1 C **2** B **3** E **4** D **5** A **6** E **7** B **8** D **9** C **10** A

Evaluate, page 23

Answers will vary.